What Happens Next?
DEALING WITH LIFE CHANGES

What Happens When I Have Dyslexia?

Emiliya King

PowerKiDS press

Published in 2026 by The Rosen Publishing Group, Inc.
2544 Clinton Street, Buffalo, NY 14224

Copyright © 2026 by The Rosen Publishing Group, Inc.

First Edition

All rights reserved. No part of this book may be reproduced in any form without permission in writing from the publisher, except by a reviewer.

Editor: Caitie McAneney
Book Design: Leslie Taylor

Photo Credits: Cover Nanci Santos Iglesias/Shutterstock.com; p. 5 Skolova/Shutterstock.com; p. 7 E.Va/Shutterstock.com; p. 9 PeopleImages.com - Yuri A/Shutterstock.com; p. 11 Pavlova Yuliia/Shutterstock.com; p. 13 PeopleImages.com - Yuri A/Shutterstock.com; p. 15 epiximages/Shutterstock.com, (inset) ShelleyAdams/File:OpenDyslexic3Regular-sample.svg_commons.wikimedia.org; p. 17 Rido/Shutterstock.com; p. 19 Igor Link/Shutterstock.com, (inset) Kathy Hutchins_Shutterstock.com; p. 21 Maryshot/Shutterstock.com.

Cataloging-in-Publication Data
Names: King, Emiliya author
Title: What happens when I have dyslexia? / Emiliya King.
Description: New York : PowerKids Press, [2026] | Series: What happens next? Dealing with life changes | Includes index.
Identifiers: LCCN 2025012741 (print) | LCCN 2025012742 (ebook) | ISBN 9781499452587 library binding | ISBN 9781499452570 paperback | ISBN 9781499452594 ebook
Subjects: LCSH: Dyslexia–Juvenile literature
Classification: LCC LB1050.5 .K46 2026 (print) | LCC LB1050.5 (ebook) | DDC 371.91/44–dc23/eng/20250410
LC record available at https://lccn.loc.gov/2025012741
LC ebook record available at https://lccn.loc.gov/2025012742
Manufactured in the United States of America

Some of the images in this book illustrate individuals who are models. The depictions do not imply actual situations or events.

CPSIA Compliance Information: Batch #CSPK26. For Further Information contact Rosen Publishing at 1-800-237-9932.

CONTENTS

Trouble with Reading............4
What Is Dyslexia?...............6
Hard Work.....................8
Getting a Diagnosis............10
Support in School.............12
Things That Help..............14
Focus on Growth..............16
No Shame....................18
The Good News...............20
Glossary.....................22
For More Information.........23
Index........................24

Trouble with Reading

Do you have trouble reading? Have you been put in a special reading group because you read slower than other kids in your class? Reading isn't always easy. Many kids struggle to learn to read.

Many things need to happen in order to read a story or understand written ideas. You need to understand how sounds make words. You need to identify printed letters. You need to connect the sounds to the letters. When issues happen with these steps, reading and understanding ideas can feel impossible.

Your Point of View

Phonics is a way of learning to read that matches sounds with letters or groups of letters in the alphabet.

Learning how speech sounds make up words is called phonemic awareness.

What Is Dyslexia?

Sometimes people who struggle with reading have dyslexia. This is a kind of learning **disability** that makes it hard for people to process written words.

Scientists have taken pictures of the brains of people with and without dyslexia. They found that people with dyslexia use different parts of their brain when reading. It makes phonemic awareness and phonics hard. Reading might seem like slow, hard work. You may struggle to read or write letters in the correct order.

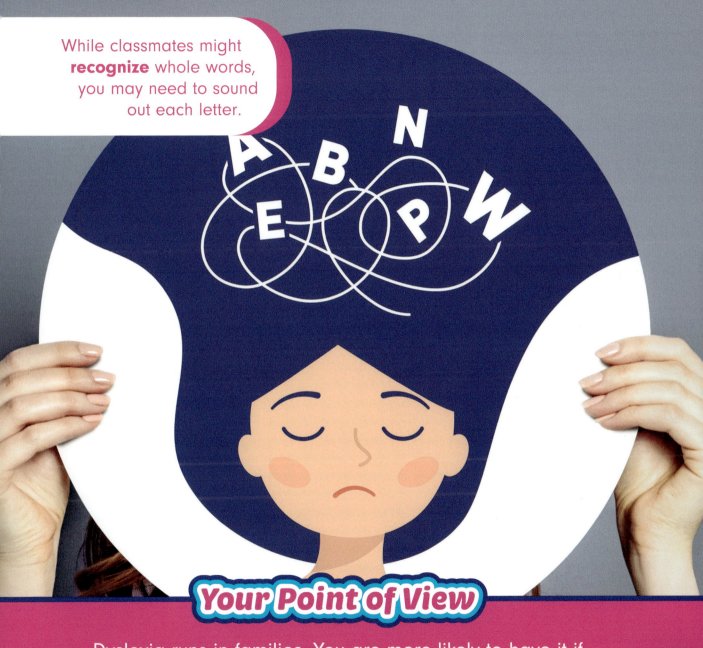

While classmates might **recognize** whole words, you may need to sound out each letter.

Your Point of View

Dyslexia runs in families. You are more likely to have it if someone in your family has it.

Hard Work

Reading with dyslexia may seem impossible or like too much work. You may feel that you're not as smart as others in your class. You may want to give up. However, it's important to ask for the help you need.

Be honest with your teachers about your reading struggles. Tell them what it's like to try to read and let them know you're trying your hardest. They can help you gain new reading skills. They may also connect you to a reading specialist to test you for dyslexia.

Your Point of View

Advocating for yourself means letting people know what you need. It is an important life skill.

Reading with dyslexia may be a challenge, but it's possible for you to read and write well with practice and support.

Getting a Diagnosis

Your school may have a reading specialist. **Psychologists** and your doctor may also be able to spot the signs of dyslexia. They can give you some tests to find out if you have dyslexia.

If you are **diagnosed** with dyslexia, you can get the help you need. Many kids are diagnosed with dyslexia in elementary school. However some kids aren't diagnosed until high school or later. The sooner you are diagnosed, the most support you can get to learn how to read and succeed in school.

You may feel upset about your diagnosis. You may feel better because you have an answer to your struggles. All feelings are okay.

Your Point of View

Around 10 to 20 percent of people have dyslexia. It is very common!

Support in School

Having dyslexia does not mean you won't be able to read. It just means you may need extra support in school. You may work with a reading specialist, special education teacher, or tutor. They can teach you tools and tips to make reading accessible, or doable.

Some students with dyslexia may have an Individualized Education Program (IEP). That helps you **achieve** learning goals with extra help. Some students with dyslexia can have extra time for tests and assignments or a reader for their tests.

Practice reading at home and at school. Over time, it will get easier.

Your Point of View

Some kids have issues with writing, called dysgraphia, or issues with math, called dyscalculia.

Things That Help

There are many people who can help you deal with your dyslexia. There are also tools and tips that can help. Find books at your reading level, especially ones with subjects that interest you. **Audiobooks** can jumpstart your love of stories, even as you work on your reading skills.

Tell your teacher if you struggle with reading aloud to the class. Organize, or order, your ideas and thoughts into visuals such as charts or webs. Ask about dyslexia-friendly **fonts** for your reading and assignments, such as Dyslexie and OpenDyslexic.

Your Point of View

Some people with dyslexia use speech-to-text **software** to get their ideas down.

Work on phonics skills using flashcards.

OpenDyslexic font

Focus on Growth

Dyslexia has nothing to do with intelligence. You are smart even if you have trouble reading at the same level as your classmates. If you focus on growth, you can achieve your goals.

There are two ways to think about intelligence. Fixed mindset is the belief that your intelligence is fixed, or unable to change. Growth mindset is the belief that you can grow in intelligence. You may need to work harder in some subjects, but you can still grow with time and effort.

It may not feel fair that you have to work harder at reading than other people. It's okay to feel **frustrated**.

Try to keep a can-do attitude when it comes to reading. Celebrate your small achievements.

No Shame

You may feel embarrassed about your dyslexia. Reading in front of others or getting a bad grade on a test can cause feelings of **shame**. However, there's no shame in having this condition. It's just one part of who you are.

You can choose to tell your friends and classmates about your dyslexia. You can explain that your brain just works differently when it comes to reading. You can also share with them the things that you are good at, or the things that interest you.

Your Point of View

When you work to overcome a great challenge or setback, that's called resilience.

Many famous people have dyslexia, including Cher (a singer), Anderson Cooper (a journalist), and Keanu Reeves (an actor).

Keanu Reeves

The Good News

Dyslexia can make it difficult to read long books or take tests within a set time. You may find it hard to understand **complex** directions or write down your ideas.

However, there's good news. With the right supports and skills, most kids with dyslexia learn to read. They learn **strategies** that help them learn alongside their peers. Practice is important, so finding books that you like can help you stay **motivated**. Confidence is important too. Be confident in your ability to grow and learn!

Your Point of View

Confidence means believing in yourself and what you can do, even if it's hard.

Some people with dyslexia practice reading aloud by reading to pets!

21

Glossary

achieve: To get by effort.

audiobook: A recorded book that is read aloud.

complex: Having many parts.

diagnose: To identify a disease by its signs and symptoms.

disability: A condition that impairs or limits a person's ability to do certain tasks or participate in daily activities.

font: A set of type or characters all of one style.

frustrated: Feeling angered, annoyed, or let down.

motivated: Having a reason and a drive to do something.

psychologist: A person who studies psychology, or the science or study of the mind.

recognize: To identify something by its features.

shame: A feeling that something is wrong with you or that you've done something wrong.

software: Programs that run on computers and perform certain functions.

strategy: A plan of action to achieve a goal.

For More Information

Books

Levy, Janey. *What Happens When I Have a Learning Difference?* Buffalo, NY: PowerKids Press, 2025.

Tolli, Jenna. *Education Matters*. Buffalo, NY: PowerKids Press, 2024.

Websites

Dyslexia
kidshealth.org/en/kids/dyslexia.html
Learn more about dyslexia and how you can cope with your diagnosis.

Understanding Dyslexia
www.youtube.com/watch?v=BOn4DWBNdOU
Watch this video that highlights five facts about dyslexia.

Publisher's note to educators and parents: Our editors have carefully reviewed these websites to ensure that they are suitable for students. Many websites change frequently, however, and we cannot guarantee that a site's future contents will continue to meet our high standards of quality and educational value. Be advised that students should be closely supervised whenever they access the internet.

Index

A
advocating, 8
audiobooks, 14

D
diagnosis, 10, 11
dyscalculia, 13
dysgraphia, 13

F
families, 7
fonts, 14

G
growth mindset, 16

I
Individualized Education Program (IEP), 12
intelligence, 16

L
learning disability, 6

P
phonemic awareness, 5, 6
phonics, 5, 6, 15
psychologist, 10

R
reading specialist, 8, 10, 12
Reeves, Keanu, 19
resilience, 18

S
software, 15
strategies, 20
support, 9, 10, 12, 20